CHAMPAGNE CHARLIE
AND LADY JAYNE

CHAMPAGNE CHARLIE AND LADY JAYNE

JESSIE LARMAN

Carnarvon Art Studio

Copyright © 2021 by Jessie Larman
First Edition: Carnarvon Art Studio

All rights reserved. This book is copyright. Apart from any fair dealing for the purpose of private study, research, criticism or review, as permitted under the Copyright Act, no part of this book may be reproduced or transmitted in any form or by any means, electronic or mechanical, including photocopying, recording or by any information storage and retrieval systems without written permission from the publisher. Enquiries should be made to the publisher.

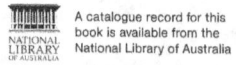
A catalogue record for this book is available from the National Library of Australia

National Library of Australia
ISBN:978-0-6450891-2-7 (paperback)
ISBN: 978-0-6450891-3-4 (ebook)
Printed and Distributed in Australia /Overseas by Ingram

Talking over the fence

Contents

1	Champagne Charlie & Lady Jayne	2
2	Girl in The Blue Dress	8
3	Talking over the Fence	13
4	The Horses have an Adventure	16
5	Home to Confess	19
6	The Hunt	22
7	Stuck	25
8	Also Stuck	27
9	Help Arrives	29
10	Follow that Horse	32
11	Back Home	37
12	Getting Ready for the Big Race	40
13	The Race	45
14	Celebrations	49

Introduction

This is the story of two beautiful horse's that fall in love.

I have written this book for all my young friends that care for Horse's.

Also in memory of our Danny Horse, who ran away, never to be found but we have not forgotten him. He was running with a pack on one of the Sheep Stations in the North of Western Australia, so we hope he is well and Happy.

Best Wishes
from Nanna Jessie.

* * *

Mrs Little with Lady Jayne

I

Champagne Charlie & Lady Jayne

Lady Jayne looked over her corral railings to the next door neighbours property, just a Lady-like look so that no-one would even know she had peeped over. What made her look was this gallop of hooves down the driveway, she saw to her surprise a great big horse with a beautiful light colour coat, almost a champagne colour she thought. Not that Lady Jayne was used to drinking champagne but she remembered the colour from the little glasses of drink that her Master and Mistress had when they said they would drink a toast to her after she had won a big race. Then it had not seemed any effort to her at the time to win, although lately she hadn't been in many races.

It seemed that they were keeping her to run in the really big race of the season next year. So most of her time was spent in training and daydreaming. She liked to daydream, sometimes it would be a dream that she was the most beautiful of all fillies, then she would toss her head up high and canter around her paddock.

Having a paddock all to herself she became very lonely at times, so the daydreaming came in very handy and passed away the time much quicker for her. Sometimes she would dream that a beautiful Stallion would come and claim her for his wife and that they would gallop together to the end of the world. What was the end of the world like she sometimes wondered, did you fall off the edge when you got there, were there lush paddocks to graze in, what were the trees like? Often she wondered this and would go off into quite a long daydream and would come to, with a jump almost, when her Mistress would be calling her name to saddle her up.

Still at the moment, she was more pre-occupied with wondering about her new neighbour, yes, he looked like a truly beautiful Stallion.

He was not like the one in her daydreams that she would want to gallop to the end of the world with - but he held himself magnificently and she could see as he passed her corral that his eyes looked quickly and almost shyly at her as he galloped past.

When this new horse was installed in his corral he could see Lady Jayne but was too far away to talk to her, so as a polite gesture he flicked his tail to say good-day to her and was surprised to see her blink her eye in such a coy manner. This he thought looks like a nice Filly. I wonder if she will talk to me when we are in our paddocks, that's if they are next to each other, which he assumed they would be as the two properties joined with a communal track between them. He looked over again at Lady Jayne and noticed that she had a delightful figure, a very graceful dark brown, almost black body with a shiny black mane and tail, she looked a bit lonely he thought and he knew he just has to get to know her better.

There was no opportunity however that day, as his new owners were busy settling him in and showing him off to their friends.

"What do you think of him my dear" Colonel Black asked his wife Bertha "isn't he a beauty?" Then he said "he is yours my dear, a present for your Birthday from me, to show how much I love you for all the years we have been so happily married together"

"But darling" said Bertha, "he must have cost you a fortune, you shouldn't have. You know I love you without you giving me an expensive gift like this"

"Ah but he is also an investment my dear" said the Colonel. "We should be able to race him, he certainly looks a winner"!

"Well, yes he does darling, he stands so well and looks so smart and is such a gorgeous colour - sort of a champagne colour don't you think?"

"Er, yes dear" replied the Colonel. "Would you like to choose a name for him, I'm sure you could choose one better than I can, after all he is your birthday present. If you think he reminds you of champagne why not call him just that?"

"Champagne, my dear, Champagne, no I couldn't possibly, after all he isn't a bottle of drink" she said with a little giggle! "Wait a minute though, what about Champagne Charlie, yes, Champagne Charlie that sounds just right for him - yes, that's what we shall name him"

So that was to be his name in future and he nodded his head in approval.

All the time that he had been listening to what his new Master and Mistress was saying; he was also looking at them and wondering what sort of people they would be to look after him? Would they be kind to him and give him enough to eat? He had heard so many awful stories about some of his companions who had not only been ill treated and whipped but who had also been half starved as well. There was his poor friend Jack who had gone to an awful family and in the end had gone away with some people called the R.S.P.C.A. he didn't really know what that meant but he knew they looked after poor horses, old horses and ill treated ones as well as those that were ill. He knew his friend Jack was safe and happy now as one of the others had whispered to him as he left his old stable with Colonel Black.

They told him Jack had a new Mistress, a little girl who loved him very much and rode him every day to give him good exercise.

Charlie looked at his Master, he looked a good sort of man, surely if I behave myself as a horse should and especially win a race for him, he may be pleased with me and treat me right. Then looking at his Mistress he noticed that she had such a happy looking face and looked so kind, he knew in his heart that he was indeed a lucky horse to be there and she would never, never ill treat him.

Suddenly Charlie felt very happy, yes this was his new home and he knew he had struck lucky in having such good people buy him. He gave a little snort and 'My Dear' patted his nose and kissed him, yes - he was definitely home!

Charlie had another look around him, it was quite a big corral, being made mostly of thick round iron piping for a fence and at one end a covered part for him as a small shelter from the weather. Also in the shelter he noticed a big drum - whatever was that and a smaller one, what on earth was it? He went to have a look and immediately heard 'Darling' say "look my dear - Champagne Charlie has gone to see if we have put any food out for him"

So that was what the big drum was for! - Looking inside it Charlie could see a smaller drum in the top of the big one, like a bowl in fact, so that it was the right height for him to eat from. The smaller drum beside the big drum was already full of water so he had a good drink straight away.

He pricked up his ears to hear Colonel Black say "Good Chap, drink up, you can't have your feed yet though boy, have to wait you know, till feeding time. We can't start to spoil you by letting you eat between meals now, can we?"

Then Colonel Black and his wife Bertha both turned to greet their friends who had started to arrive for Mrs. Black's Birthday Tea.

One of the guests was a young teenager. "Goodness" thought Charlie, "haven't I seen that girl before somewhere - but where?"

* * *

Girl in the Blue Dress

2

Girl in The Blue Dress

Champagne Charlie closed his eyes and thought and thought, still he could not think where or when he had seen this pretty girl in her blue dress. "Wait a minute" thought Charlie, blue dress, of course she was the one he had rescued nearly a year ago. She was wearing a blue dress then, that's how he had been able to see her, yes he could remember it all now. He thought back nearly a year to when he was out playing hide and seek with his friends in the paddocks where they had been put out to grass. They were very big paddocks, all in all about a couple of thousand acres of bush and scrub. Some of the trees were just big enough and bushy enough to hide behind. So Charlie and his friends used to hide. Then one horse would be chosen to look for them, who-ever was found first would then have his turn to search for the others, which of course had to find new hiding places each time they had a new horse to look out and find them. Everyone would come out of hiding when the first one was found and neigh very loudly and laugh because they had been clever enough not to be caught.

Now it was on one of Charlie's turns at being the one to find them, that he thought he heard a human voice calling, yes, there it was again, what did it say, "help, help I'm slipping" then a terrible scream and a big splash. !

Whatever was going on didn't seem far away, just behind a few trees to the left of him. He knew that it was humans playing and the voice sounded very frightened. Listen what was that? another voice crying out "help, help, someone please come"

Champagne Charlie galloped quickly to the left of him and there behind those trees he saw an awful sight, someone in the water was flapping their arms up and down and trying to hold on to a broken piece of branch. The water was very deep, it was a Dam that the Farmer used for irrigation of his property and for watering his Stock. Although he didn't know at the time the Dam was fifty foot deep at the centre, Charlie galloped to the edge just in time to see a girl in a blue dress get a firm hold on to the floating branch.

On the bank of the Dam was a young lad named Christopher, when he saw Charlie horse he called out "good horse, please help Sally, she can't swim very well and neither can I, please fetch her out of the water"

Much to Christopher's surprise, Charlie horse understood exactly what was wanted and without a thought for his own safety stepped carefully into the water and swan out to Sally where she had floated away from the side. Sally caught hold of his mane and then put her arms around Charlie's neck. After waiting to make sure she had a proper hold on his neck, Charlie swam to the side where Sally managed to grab hold of the bamboo cane that was growing half in and half out of the water. Seeing her safely ashore Charlie tried to get out but the bank was too steep, what was he to do, he neighed at the children who were hugging each other with relief that Sally was safe. Sally being so grateful to be safe and Christopher so happy she was out, that for the moment they had forgotten him. "Look" said Christopher "the horse can't get out, it's too deep at the edge for him. There must be a shallow place somewhere near the edge surely"

"I know" said Sally, shivering with cold in her wet clothes, "remember over there by that big Eucalyptus tree where we used to play monsters, he could get out there - let us call him and see if he will follow us around to it."

So Christopher called "horse, horse, come over here" and started to run in the direction of the old Eucalyptus tree. At first Champagne Charlie wondered what the boy was shouting about and continued pawing at the edge, trying to get out. However, when Christopher reached the tree he started calling again, "come on horse you can get out here, come on, oh! come on! or you will drown"

Sally was still standing near Charlie horse who was getting rather anxious, not knowing what to do, so she pointed to Christopher and said kindly to Charlie, "come on go to Christopher and you will be able to get out". She walked along a little way and then came back to him, then she started to walk towards Christopher again calling to Charlie, "come on horse, good boy, good boy, come on," Suddenly Charlie realized they were trying to help him, so he swam along to the big tree and got a footing on the bank of the Dam, he managed to pull himself out because the bank went up steadily by the tree roots.

He stood and shook water everywhere, then got a bit of a fright as both children threw their arms around him and kissed him, they kept on thanking him and hugging him.

Then suddenly he thought, "my goodness all my friends will still be hiding, waiting for me to catch them". So he shook himself free of the children and galloped back to play hide and seek with his friends.

He had often wondered if the girl was alright and now was quite surprised to be standing in his new home looking at her wondering if in turn she would remember him. He need not have worried because she came straight up to him and said "Hello horse, you must be the one that saved me from drowning, yes you must be I remember, you had a little dark brown mark under your mane, let me lift up your mane and see. Yes, there it is, you darling horse, Mummy, Daddy come quickly, this is the horse that saved me last year. Do you think we could have him, please ask if they will let us buy him?" "No dear" said Daddy, Colonel Black has just bought him as a birthday present for Mrs. Black, we certainly can't ask him to sell him the day he has bought him!'

"What's this" asked Colonel Black overhearing the last part of the conversation, "sell him?, you must be joking, he is a Champion, he is going to be trained to win the big race next year"

"But he saved me from drowning Colonel Black" said Sally, "please let me have him, please"

"Oh, no my dear young lady but I'll tell you what, you can come and ride him in my paddocks when ever you like, if he is that precious to you, would you like that?" asked Colonel Black.

Sally thought a moment then she said "I should be very pleased to Colonel Black, after all it's wrong of me ask for someone else's birthday present isn't it"?

So it was settled. Sally came over as often as she could, which was usually once a week, because being a school girl, she had a lot of homework to do and could only find time to come on a Friday after school. Which was just right really as Christopher lived next door and rode and exercised "Lady Jayne" on the same evenings. They used to meet each other down the paddock and talk over the fence, while still on their horses. Also being teenagers now, Sally thirteen and Christopher fourteen they found much to talk about. Christopher had been amazed to find that Champagne Charlie was the horse that had rescued Sally.

* * *

Talking over the fence

They jumped over the fence together

3

Talking over the Fence

Early one Friday evening Sally and Christopher met at the fence as usual, they both cantered up to their favourite spot under a large Eucalyptus tree. The two horses were always glad of a rest from their exercise and stopped to nibble the sweet grass under foot.

"Do you realize" said Sally "that we have been meeting here for about three months now. Charlie knows that when I have exercised him all around the paddock it is time to come over to our spot"

"It's funny you should say that" replied Christopher because Lady Jayne makes her way straight here after her gallop. I walk her around first as you know, then trot, canter and gallop, then she just turns her head and starts coming over here. I think they are quite fond of each other. Have you noticed the way they look sometimes when we are together? Lady Jayne looks so shy whenever Charlie throws his head back and shakes his mane, I am sure he is asking her if she likes him."

Now the children of course didn't realize that the two horses understood what they were saying and were quite surprised, Sally especially, when Champagne Charlie stopped nibbling the grass, threw back his head and shook his mane - looking at Lady Jayne as he did so. But what was this, Lady Jayne took one look at him and carried on eating the grass. She was quite overcome and embarrassed because she had been keeping her feelings to herself, so she had thought. Lady Jayne was thinking how much she had come to adore this magnificent beast who lived next door and went straight into one of her daydreams of galloping off with him to the end of the world.

Suddenly, she felt her young Master give a tug on her reins, "I know, what about this Sally" said Christopher, "we will jump the fence and give you a race to the water-hole about a kilometer away over there, the two horses have never had a race together. My Parents have gone to the races with Colonel and Mrs. Black so they won't miss us, what do you say?" "Oh, I don't think we ought to you know, we should get into dreadful trouble if we were found out" replied Sally. "Come on" Christopher called, riding away, "don't be a sissy, Charlie can easily jump the fence at the bottom" and with that he started to gallop Lady Jayne further down his own paddock to the fence at the bottom.

Sally decided to follow, so she and Charlie galloped along to catch them up. Eventually they reached the fence at the same time as Lady Jayne and Christopher and all jumped together. Then the race was on. Holding tightly on to the reins of the horses both teenagers urged their horses on with words of encouragement.

"Good girl Lady Jayne come on" called Christopher, while Sally kept saying "beat them Charlie - go on, go on"

They were still neck and neck when a small salt bush appeared in Charlies track, instead of going round it Sally got him to jump over, this lost them a bit of time, therefore Lady Jayne had pulled away in front of them. "Come on Charlie, we have to catch up" Sally said as she pulled on his reins, "we can't let a Lady Horse beat you" so Charlie galloped as fast as he could, caught the others up and passed them in good time for him to reach the waterhole first.

"Well-done Sally" gasped Christopher dismounting, "you did well to beat us like that, it certainly was an exciting race. I tell you what, lets sit down and rest over there in the shade of that big old tree, if we take the horses saddles off they can have a rest too. Also they may like a drink from the waterhole, yes, look we can tether them out just over there" So they tethered them out near the edge of the water and took off the saddles. Then Sally and Christopher flopped down on the cool earth under the large old Gum tree, they were exhausted.

4

The Horses have an Adventure

While they were having a drink Champagne Charlie looked at Lady Jayne and thought how beautiful she looked, her coat so shiny after running, looked almost black and very soft, her big eyes looked up at that moment just in time to see him watching her.

They looked into each others eyes and knew that they had fallen in love. Charlie nuzzled her with his nose and Lady Jayne almost fainted with happiness. It's not a dream, she kept telling herself, it's not a dream, he really does like me. If only we were free to go off together it would be so wonderful. Charlie looked at her again and she thought he knew what she must be thinking so she put her nose next to his and this time gave him a nuzzle.

Sally sat up just in time to see them, "Christopher, look aren't they just beautiful, they must like each other. Do you see the way Lady Jayne was nuzzling Charlie? By the way I think we ought to be going back now as it will take us a while to brush the horses down to-night."

"Alright, you be untying them while I sort these saddles out, we shouldn't have thrown them down in such a heap"

"Right-o" replied Sally, I'll fetch the horses over while you un-muddle the saddles. Come on Lady Jayne and Charlie we are going home now. Let's untie you so Christopher can saddle up for us."

However it appeared that Lady Jayne had other ideas, for as soon as Sally had the bridle in her hand Lady Jayne pulled hard and got away, she turned just for an instant to look at Charlie and neighed for him to follow her. She knew she was doing wrong but she had dreamed so often of falling in love with such a handsome horse as Charlie that she felt she must go and knew in her heart that he would follow her. Yes, he did, he also pulled away from Sally, rearing up as he did so and then galloping after his true love.

They raced along at a tremendous speed, past the old trees and over small hillocks, on and on they ran, faster and faster. Lady Jayne could feel the evening wind in her mane. She felt free, she was free at last and in pursuit came Champagne Charlie, just close behind her. Now a few more of his superb strides and he was galloping beside her. On and on they went, neither of them looking back. Into the sunset of the evening, past an old windmill, still going around, past another waterhole they sped.

They must have travelled quite a few kilometers before Lady Jayne started to slow down to a canter, then to a trot, with Charlie still beside her. What a handsome pair they made with her dark body next to Charlie's light colour one, trotting along in the last light of the evening.

At last they stopped by a small water hole and both horses drank long and deep from the cool water. Then happily Charlie turned and tossing his fine head, gave Lady Jayne a little nip on her neck. Yes she was a fine horse he thought, giving her a loving look. Charlie was sure now that he would like her for his wife and decided he would wait till they both got their breath back after the long run before telling her so.

* * *

5

Home to Confess

Sally and Christopher couldn't believe their eyes, both horses racing away from them, what could they do?

"It's all my fault" Sally lamented, "I should have held on tighter to Lady Jayne but she just seemed to pull away so hard, then Charlie - well, he just tugged his reins out of my hand, what could I do.? Oh! Christopher whatever will they say when we get back. Not only that, however are we going to get back with these saddles to carry, it's going to take ages"

"Don't turn on the water works Sally, it's not really your fault, it's just one of those things, come on, it's no good going after them it will be dark soon, we just better try getting back"

Now, it's one thing to ride a horse a few kilometers and quite another to walk back the same distance carrying a saddle etc.,

Anyway, with quite a few misgivings, Sally picked up her saddle and followed after Christopher who thought they had better get started. It was only just over two kilometers to their houses but it seemed like they were walking forever. Christopher apologized to Sally for not being able to help carry her saddle and also for suggesting the race in the first place. Eventually they were at the fence to the paddocks. They put the saddles on the ground and Christopher climbed over the fence, then Sally passed him up the saddles which he put on the ground beside him . It didn't take Sally a minute to climb over the fence and then they carried on together to Christopher's house.

When they reached the next fence they could see lots of lights in the distance near the house, as by this time the sun had gone down and it was dark.

"Oh dear!" said Christopher "they are back from the races, goodness knows what they will say"

As it happened they had plenty to say. First of all Christopher's Father asked where the devil they had been? Then after listening to Christopher's story, realizing they had come back without the horses, was speechless for the moment.

Christopher's Mother managed to get a word in to ask "where on earth could the horse's be now?"

"I honestly don't know" her Son replied "but we thought it best to come straight home then look for them when it gets light. You see they went so quickly we never had a chance to catch them"

"Why on earth did you do such a stupid thing in the first place" asked his Father, "two valuable race horses, fancy getting them to jump the fence, let alone race against each other. Come on we better go next door and confess to Colonel Black. I can't say he'll be very pleased at the news, they have already been round once to ask if we knew where Sally and Charlie were. I told him you were probably still talking down the paddock,.....Christopher bring Sally's saddle for her and let's get it over with"

Colonel Black, however, didn't take things as calmly as his neighbour, he banged his fist on the table and told them that they were totally irresponsible and that at first light they could jolly well help in the search. He would get the Army out if necessary, yes and the Airforce, he wasn't going to let next years winner of the cup slip through his fingers just like that.

* * *

Going home to confess

6

The Hunt

By four-thirty next morning it was starting to get light. Colonel Black was already up and dressed, pacing up and down in the lounge room. The kettle whistled in the kitchen and he went through to make a cup of tea, deciding at the same time to wake his wife Bertha as she could help organize food and drink ready for the hunt to find the horses.

Bertha however could not seem to wake up, so when Colonel Black took her in a cup of tea he gave her a gentle shake. "Come along dear, Wakey - Wakey, we have to get off to an early start." Bertha turned over and opened one eye, looked at the clock and put her head back on the pillow. "Don't go back to sleep my dear we have to look for the horses" said the Colonel.

"Oh! goodness me yes" Bertha exclaimed, "what am I thinking? I should be up. Thank you for my cup of tea darling I'll be with you in a minute. Can I smell the bacon cooking"?

"Yes you can my dear" said Colonel Black, rushing out of the bedroom, "it should be cooked by now, I will put your egg in the pan Bertha so be quick"

After a hurried meal of egg, bacon, toast and coffee, Mrs. Black packed some sandwiches to take on the hunt. Just as they were ready a knock came on the door, it was their neighbours who were also ready to go, with Christopher in the jeep looking decidedly guilty still.

Colonel and Mrs. Black greeted them and walked over to their own four wheel drive. Mrs. Black was putting the picnic lunch in the back when a voice called, "wait for me, wait for me" it was Sally running as fast as she could in case they went without her. "Get in dear" said Mrs. Black kindly, she knew Sally must be

feeling very bad about the horses getting away. "We shall drive around to the end of the paddocks then you can tell us which way to go for the best to look for Charlie and Lady Jayne" "Alright Mrs. Black, thank you for letting me come" Sally said. She didn't dare to look at Christopher in case she started crying again.

At the bottom of the paddock, the children showed them where they had jumped over the fence, then about one kilometer further on where the horses may have raced to and stopped for a drink.

"That was the way they headed off" volunteered Christopher pointing in the direction that the horses had gone.

"Sit down Christopher" said his father Mr. Little, don't get so excited standing up like that while we are moving."

"I'm aright Father" Christopher said, still standing, holding onto the overhead support in their topless jeep, "I can see better like this."

"Hold on then, lets stop and have a word with Colonel Black, it may be better to split up." With that he honked on his horn to attract Colonel Blacks attention and signaled him to stop.

Without getting out of his jeep, Mr. Little shouted to the Colonel, "I say old Chap it would be a good idea if we split up, we've got our Walkie-Talkies so can keep in touch with each other, what do you think?"

"Well it's worth a try" said the Colonel, "they could be anywhere, possibly miles away by now, yes, alright then, we'll split up. We'll go over on that track, you go straight ahead, you may come to a waterhole. I bet that's where we shall find them, somewhere near a waterhole. Anyway I know a waterhole along this track to my left, it's about ten kilometers further on, so I will give you a buzz when we get there."

With that he shot forward at an alarming pace and Sally and Mrs. Black were thrown up in the air off their seats.

"Mad fool" grumbled Mr. Little "serve him right if he goes into something driving at that rate."

* * *

7

Stuck

After much hectic driving on the unmade almost non existent road, Mr. Little stopped his car, turned to his wife and Christopher saying "look here, the Colonel hasn't bothered to give us a buzz. I suppose he hasn't found them at the waterhole he mentioned and has gone on, thinking he will find them before us. Goodness only knows where there is a waterhole up here, we must have covered over fifty kilometers by now and not a sign of them. The horses wouldn't have come all this way I'm sure, I'll give the Colonel buzz. I think then we'll turn back and take another track. Would you get the drink out Rose while I talk to him."

"Hello, hello, come in please" shouted Mr. Little into his C.B. Radio. No answer came. So he tried again and again without success.

"Here you are John" said his wife, "have a drink, here is yours Christopher as well. Leave the set switched on John while you drink, maybe they will get through to us while we have a break"

"Mum can I have a couple of sandwiches please" asked Christopher. "I couldn't eat any breakfast, now I'm starving hungry" "Of course you can, help yourself dear, they are in the Esky, make sure you cover it up afterwards because of the flies"

"Will you two stop nattering" Mr. Little said in a loud voice, I can hear something on here. Whatever is that old fool saying?"

"Sounds as if he is swearing" said Christopher, "he sounds pretty mad, tell you what Dad, shout at him through this end, he may hear you if he stops going on long enough"

Mr. Little gave Christopher an annoyed look, picked up his mouth piece and shouted "Colonel Black can you hear me, come in please"

After a few of these calls a voice answered, it was Mrs. Black. "Hello it's Bertha here, we are stuck, can you help, we are stuck in sand, need towing out, we are about 13 kilometers off the turning where we left you, please hurry, over and out"

"Hello Bertha, it's John here, be with you in about an hour, over and out"

"Well, well, that will teach the silly old goat a lesson, fancy getting himself stuck in the sand, thought he knew better than that".

"Don't go on so John, lets hurry back, it's getting very hot now the sun is up:" his wife exclaimed.

8

Also Stuck

At the waterhole a couple of kilometers further on from where the Colonel had got stuck, two beautiful horses were eating their breakfast of soft green grass by the edge of the water, in fact it was the only bit of green grass for hundreds of kilometers.

Yes, they had come to a stop after their long gallop last night and decided to stay there by the waterhole together. As the stars had come out Charlie had plucked up courage to tell Lady Jayne he loved her and that he would like her to be his wife. Lady Layne accepted and they had nuzzled each other and looked into each others eyes with out a thought even of their young master and mistress being worried about them.

This being morning, Champagne Charlie began to think of his good home with Colonel Black and thought how he would miss seeing Sally each day and being ridden and groomed, also his good food.

As much as he loved Lady Jayne he thought they would both be better off if they went back home to their respective owners.

How could he tell her this especially so soon after galloping away together, no, he would just have to wait but could see that in the harsh countryside they would certainly have a hard time of it.

Lady Jayne was having a long drink and was off into one of her daydreams again.

Such a beautiful creature Charlie thought but she hasn't any brains. I shall have to get her back somehow. Just then Lady Jayne slipped, her front right hoof which was steading her as she drank the cool water, sank down suddenly in the soft clay and sand. She fell awkwardly onto her side, try as she would she could not get up. Charlie went nearer and pushed with his head to help her roll over but she was well and truly stuck. "Oh dear" he thought "what shall I do?"

Lady Jayne neighed loudly in protest and floundered about but for some reason she couldn't get back on her feet and appeared to be sinking in the soft sand.

Charlie neighed back to her and told her he would go for help. He turned around to sniff the air and then galloped off very fast in the direction they had come the night before, leaving Lady Jayne looking wistfully after him!

"Oh dear" she thought "it's all my own fault, we should never have run away in the first place"

She decided she had better stay still until his return.

* * *

9

Help Arrives

Charlie galloped on fast for a few kilometers, then slowed down to take his bearings. A road branched off to his right. Now which one did they come along last night? He couldn't remember, as it was almost dark then and things look different in the day light.

He stood on top of a little hillock and sniffed the air again, as he did so he got the scent of men. Yes, he was sure, so without more ado he was back on the roadway and took the one straight ahead. Yes, he was right, further on he could see a vehicle. He galloped faster and of course he came upon Colonel Black and Mrs. Black with Sally all sitting forlornly in the shade of the jeep.

"Shiver my timers" exclaimed the Colonel, "it's Champagne Charlie, look. it must be"! "Charlie" shouted the Colonel "come here, come on there's a good fellow"

But he needn't have worried, Charlie came up fast when he recognized everyone and went straight up to Sally who threw her arms around him and cried into his mane.

Mrs. Black stroked his neck and Colonel Black patted him on the rump saying "it's good to have you back Charlie" Then turning to his wife he said "Bertha do you know I think with Charlie's help we could get this confounded jeep out of the sand. Get the rope my dear and we will tie it to his halter then get him to pull. Sally you tie it on, quickly there's a good girl"

Charlie stood still wondering what they were going to do? As Sally put the rope on she explained to him that he was going to help them pull the jeep out of the sand.

Champagne Charlie summed up the situation quite quickly and decided this must be done before he could take the Colonel back for Lady Jayne.

When they were ready he started to pull, with Sally holding his halter and urging him on.

However, it was too much for him. Then Mrs. Black said, "look dear, why don't you un-hitch the horse float from the back then maybe he can pull us free a bit easier"

"Oh help!" groaned The Colonel I forgot about that. "Hang on Sally I'll get out and unshackle the float, he also rearranged the pieces of dead wood that he had placed under the wheels of the jeep, got back in, turned the ignition on and yelled at Sally and Charlie to 'Pull'

Charlie heaved and suddenly the jeep came out of the sand onto the firmer ground. The Colonel turned the ignition off and jumped down. "Good horse, good fellow, thank heavens we're out! Right, now give me a hand Bertha to pull the float and fasten it on again. Sally undo the rope and we'll get Charlie into the float"

When the float was fixed on Charlie wouldn't get in. "Don't tell me we are in for more trouble" said the Colonel, going red in the face, "I've just about had enough"

Just then they heard a car in the distance, "keep hold of him Sally" called the Colonel "someone is coming, we don't want him running off in a fright"

When the car came into sight they could see it was the Little's jeep. Mr. Little slowed down and came to a stop beside them quite surprised to see Charlie horse standing there and the Colonel's jeep out of the sand.

"Well you've found one horse then, what about mine, where is she" asked Mr. Little?

"How should I know" snapped the Colonel, "this one came galloping towards us from nowhere, help me get him in his float will you, he won't go in"

Both men got one each side of Charlie's halter and started to lead him to the float. Suddenly he reared up and Mr. Little went sprawling, Colonel Black pulled hard on the halter and got Charlie to stand still. He gave him another pull which made him rear up pawing the air, his magnificent mane flying behind him, he whinnied loudly and galloped of in the direction of where he had left Lady Jayne stuck in the waterhole.

* * *

10

Follow that Horse

"Oh Criky" the Colonel moaned "now look - he's gone again" He jumped into his jeep and started after him, leaving Mr. Little still brushing himself down.

"How on earth are we going to get him back Bertha, he could suddenly go bush and we shall never find him"

"Colonel" said Sally, "do you think he could be taking us to Lady Jayne, he surely would know where she is"

"Don't talk daft girl, he is just running because he doesn't want to get into the horse float"

Sally started to get excited and was pointing ahead at a waterhole where the great Stallion had stopped, he was rearing up again and then pawing the ground.

"Look, look", Sally gasped, Lady Jayne is lying in the sand, why doesn't she get up? I bet she is hurt and Charlie has brought us to help her."

"H'm" the Colonel said, as he brought the vehicle to a stop and jumped out. "H'm, maybe you're right girl, anyway that's not sand, it's more like quick sand and she has got herself bogged in it. Quick get the rope again and tie it onto Charlie's halter, he will have to pull all over again now".

Just then Mr. Little arrived "Oh my goodness, my Lady Jayne, what have you done to her?"

"We haven't done anything" Bertha told him, "we found her like this, they are tying the rope to Charlie in the hope of pulling her free but I can't see how they will fix it to her"

"Hold on Charlie" shouted Christopher, "if I lay on my stomach and crawl out to her I could probably get the rope around her neck."

"Don't you dare Christopher," said his Father, we would break her neck pulling and you may well sink into that sand. I'll tell you what, if we could get the rope under her body around the front legs, then we could pull better."

"Right, give me the rope I'm not as heavy as you" replied Christopher. "She knows me better anyway. Sally you keep hold of Charlie until I've tied the rope around Lady Jayne.

Father hold my ankles incase I start to sink, Oh! wait we've got another rope in our car, I'll put it around my own waist as a safely measure, Mum can you pass it to me please."

Christopher fastened the rope and lay down on his tummy, all the time talking to Lady Jayne who had started to become quite agitated, "It won't be long now, there's a good girl, lay still, we'll get you out, lay still now, I won't take very long to help get you out" Christopher said trying to calm her.

As soon as his body touched the sand, he felt himself start to sink but not too much. He could crawl along with the rope around his waist so with his father and Colonel Black holding the other end that gave him confidence to press on.

How he was going to get the rope around the horses body, he still had no idea. Also she had turned over and her legs were now towards him, he was sure he would never do it. He turned around saying "I am going to try standing up, keep the rope tight incase I go down"

Christopher tried to stand and found to his relief that when the wet sand reached his waist he stopped sinking. "This is better, I'll walk out to her head, go around and put the other rope under her body, if I stay by her head and do it we should stand a chance." he thought!

Mr. Little and Colonel Black were both holding the rope, keeping quiet in case they frightened Lady Jayne.

The two women - Mrs. Black and Mrs. Little were standing near the edge watching in horror in case Christopher went down.

Sally was holding on to Charlie waiting to tell him when he could pull. Charlie was starting to get restless as Christopher was taking so long to get the rope around the other horse. At last he did it and fastening it securely called to Sally to 'pull'.

"Slowly Sally, not so fast, it's not far to the edge" shouted Christopher.

But Lady Jayne remained stuck. Christopher put his hands under her to help lift but still she didn't budge.

"Come on Charlie," cried Sally, "please pull. Mrs. Black, Mrs. Little can you help pull on the rope with us, if you take the strain near the edge of the sand I'll get Charlie to give a big tug, it's the only way". So with a great heave the mighty Stallion pulled and strained on the rope and his beloved Jayne came beautifully right to the edge, rolled over and stood up. The two ladies pulling the rope had done a good job and were now picking themselves up after falling over with the pull of the rope.

Quickly the men pulled Christopher out and untied him. They all made such fuss of Lady Jayne, she stood there covered in wet sand and feeling very forlorn.

"If only" she thought, "if only I hadn't run away" and in that moment realized that she must go back home with her owners who obviously thought so much of her that they were risking their own lives trying to help her. She looked sadly at Champagne Charlie who looked at her and neighed. Then Lady Jayne started to walk with Christopher to her float. What was this, she couldn't hardly bear to put her right front leg to the ground, Oh! the pain, what had she done? Christopher bent down and gently felt her fetlock. "I think she has broken something, come along we will have to fix you up when we get you back, sorry old girl but there's not much we can do apart from putting a quick bandage around it"

Mr. Little strapped up Lady Jayne's leg and guided her into her horse float.

By this time Charlie horse had gone quietly into his horse float and Sally was busy taking off his halter, telling him what a hero he was for taking them there and getting Lady Jayne free from sinking into the sand.

She gave Charlie a kiss and got into the jeep with Colonel and Mrs. Black.

"Right" said the Colonel, "we'll take it steady going back, you go first John and set the pace, I shan't be tempted to speed along then. Thank goodness we've got them back!

* * *

Mrs Little with Lady Jayne

11

Back Home

Back home they went into their respective drives and put the horses into their own yards, filled their mangers with fresh chaff and topped up the water containers. Sally started to groom Champagne Charlie while he was eating. Meanwhile next door Mr. Little who had phoned the Vet was waiting impatiently for him to arrive to examine Lady Jayne's leg.

Christopher was trying to hose the wet sand and mud off of Lady Jayne when the Vet appeared.

"It's lucky you managed to get me on the phone Mr. Little. Now what exactly is the matter with her?" enquired the Vet.

After explaining about her leg and the fall Mr. Little took the Vet over for the examination.

"Let's see now Lady Jayne - what have you been up to? You look a bit exhausted. I think I had better give her something Mr. Little to keep her calm for a couple of days. Yes, she has definitely injured her right leg, it seems as if she has fractured or broken the cannon. You need to bring her to my surgery to be x-rayed. Can you bring her after 2pm this afternoon, not before 2pm as I am on my way to fix up Mr. Kettles brown Cow. See you later old girl," he said, giving Lady Jayne a friendly pat on her rear.

She stood there looking so forlorn, her beautiful near black coat beginning to gleam under Christopher's careful grooming. Lady Jayne held her head down as if she really was ashamed of causing so much trouble.

Off she went daydreaming again, "I shall never be able to look Champagne Charlie in the face now, Oh!, what a mess I have made of things, if only, if only, - but it's too late now!

My poor leg, it does hurt, goodness knows if I shall be able to race again. Surely they won't shoot me like they do some of the other horses. Oh! my goodness, please don't let them shoot me"

While she was daydreaming, they were arranging about the ex-ray. It was agreed that Christopher should accompany Mr. Little to the Vet's to help keep Lady Jayne calm.

Christopher jumped over the fence to see Sally who was still grooming Charlie and told her what was happening. Sally looked worried and said "you know Christopher - Lady Jayne will be lucky if she can ever run again. We had better apologize again to your Father. I feel awful about all this, come on lets get it over with."

So they both went back over the fence to look for Mr. Little, they found him sitting on an old box in one of the stables.

"Dad can we have a word with you, it's about Lady Jayne, we want to say we are truly sorry about all the trouble we have caused you, also we think we should be responsible for the Vet's fees." said Christopher, hoping his Father would not punish them too much.

"Well, well, it's a bit late to think about being sorry my boy and you Sally" said Mr. Little. "Alright girl don't start to cry, I know how you both must feel so I think we had better forget the whole affair. Sally you can come down for the ex-ray if you like, it should not take long. Now run along you two and get cleaned up, we better go in for lunch"

Lunch however in both households consisted of the picnic's they had taken with them and not eaten. No-one said much, except that Colonel Black told Sally he had forgiven her being so foolish and that she could carry on looking after Charlie if she still wanted to. Sally was overjoyed at this news and promptly got up and went over to kiss him on the cheek, much to the Colonel's embarrassment. Mrs. Black was relieved at her husbands decision and drank her cup of tea thoughtfully.

* * *

12

Getting Ready for the Big Race

Well Lady Jayne was x-rayed and her leg duly bandaged, it was not broken, much to everyone's relief, just badly sprained. But Mr. Little was told that it would be out of the question to hope that she would be better in time to race in the next big race due to take place in two months time.

He was obviously disappointed but after all, he thought 'there is always another time' Mr. Little was glad that he had his beloved horse back so didn't say too much about it. Lady Jayne was his favourite. There was no doubt about that, so he usually fussed around her nearly every day.

Over the fence the next day he watched his neighbour Colonel Black talking to Champagne Charlie telling him his chances in the race were great. Turning, Colonel Black caught sight of Mr. Little looking at him and strolled over. "Hello John how are things, how is Lady Jayne's leg today. What do you think of Charlie, looking great isn't he?"

"Yes" replied Mr. Little " he certainly is, I was watching Sally put him through his paces this morning, he is magnificent".

"Course he is, I knew he was a winner when I first saw him. I'll tell you what, now that Lady Jayne is out of the race he should certainly win. I know she has a great speed, also Lady Jayne really was the only threat to him that I could see, so I'm confident now of his chances. Can't wait to present Bertha with the trophy she will be so proud of him!"

"I shouldn't be too confident" John replied, remember pride comes before a fall and all that"

"Well I shall pretend I didn't hear you" Colonel Black retorted, "anyway how about having a flutter - put some money on him at the bookies?"

" I May even do that you know" laughed Mr. Little "he may be in the first ten horses"

"If that is all you can do, stand and make fun of him I shall go" laughed Colonel Black knowing full well that his friend had every intention of backing Champagne Charlie.

Two months went around very quickly. Sally came early evening to give Charlie Horse a good grooming, as the next day was the big day. She promised to come early next morning to groom him thoroughly again and was getting very excited as she felt he was more her horse than anyone's as she had done so much work on him.

Next morning came in a wave of excitement, Sally was at the Black's house just as it was getting light, she had already started to look after Charlie before the Colonel was out of bed.

Bertha insisted that the Colonel and Sally sit down to have a proper breakfast as the horse float wasn't coming for Charlie until 8.0am. So at 6.30am they were having egg and bacon, toast and tea while keeping one eye on the clock, you would have thought that they were in the race themselves they were all so excited.

However after eating as fast as they could, Sally and Colonel Black thanked Bertha for breakfast, then hastily went out to make Champagne Charlie look like a Champion.

Between them they brushed his coat until it shone, brushed and combed his mane also his tail, all the leather work, saddle, bridle etc., was given an extra special polish and they were only just ready when the man with the horse float came to take him to the race course. - "Do you think I could go with him and look after him there in case he gets nervous?" Sally asked. "Certainly not" replied the Colonel, "you have to come with us this afternoon and look respectable young lady, because he might just win the trophy. This is his great day and he doesn't want us interfering, do you boy" he said as he stroked Charlie gently on his nose.

They led him out of his stable and into the waiting horse float. Champagne Charlie walked in looking very majestic knowing this was his special day.

When he was stabled at the race-course he thought to himself, "Sally has been so good to me I must win for her sake, also poor Lady Jayne, she is missing out because of my foolishness, I must make it up to them. I shall try my best to run and win that trophy they keep talking about."

Afternoon came and Colonel Black went round for his friend as they were all going together to the track but Mrs. Little came to the door quite agitated "Oh dear" said Rose, John is out the back with Lady Jayne she is in some sort of pain, we are waiting for the Vet, you go on without us and we will come latter if she is alright"

"Shall I have a look at her?" asked the Colonel.

"No, no you will only make yourselves late, don't worry, the Vet promised to be here shortly" said Mrs. Little.

So off they went, Colonel and Mrs. Black also Sally each of them all dressed up just in case Champagne Charlie did happen to win the Trophy!

When they got to the race track it was crowded. They showed their special cards to go through the gate, then went into the owners and trainers stands which were separated from the public.

Having found what he thought was a good spot the Colonel asked his wife Bertha and Sally to take a seat.

They had purchased a race book with all the races in and found that Champagne Charlie was in the third race of the afternoon and was also placed number three. The Colonel thought that was a good omen and proceeded to look around the race course through his binoculars.

Suddenly the Colonel jumped up, "Bertha I forgot about putting my bet on, could you do it for me please my dear?"

"Now sit down" his wife replied "you can't put it on until it's

time for that race! ...... I wonder if Rose and John will manage to come here in time for Charlie's race?" she said.

"I wonder how Lady Jayne is thought Sally?"

* * *

Getting Ready for the Big Race

13

The Race

Christopher found Colonel and Mrs. Black in the owners and trainers stand just before the start of the second race. Having been away for the last few days he had come home specially for the race. Sally was overjoyed to see him and moved up to give him a seat next to her.

"Well this is indeed a surprise, my boy" bellowed the Colonel "glad you've come to cheer us on, what about your Parents are they on the way"

"Thought they would be here" said Christopher. "I didn't have time to go home first, I came straight here as I was late, the bus got held up in the traffic".

"Don't worry," boomed the Colonel "look - the horses are off, this is the second race, ours is the next you know, you only just made it"

The horse's flashed by with a lot of cheering, it was all over very quickly. At last the time had come for their own race.

"Here comes Mum and Dad" Christopher shouted above the racket. "Over here Mum," he waved like mad but they couldn't see him. He turned to the Colonel but he had disappeared, "where has he gone Sally, he better be quick"

"Sit down dear" said Mrs. Black "don't get so excited, he's only gone to put his bet on. Where are your Parents Christopher, I can't see them? It's alright, we may as well find them later or we shall all get lost. I know you saw them down there so at least we know they are here" she said.

"Well I've put my shirt on him" gasped the Colonel when he came back sitting down heavily next to his wife, "lets hope he is at least third so I get some money back"

"You haven't got cold feet darling about him winning, now surely after all you have been saying about him" asked Mrs. Black.?

Colonel Black replied, "Well, I have a funny sort of feeling now the time has come. After all, my dear, this is our first big race you know as well as Charlie's. Look they are lining them up, our young Jockey looks very smart. Doesn't his chocolate coloured silk shirt look good against Charlie's light colour coat. The number three shows up well in silver material on the back of the Jockey's shirt too I reckon Bertha"

"I should really be the jockey" said Sally quietly. The Colonel didn't hear her but Christopher did. "Don't be like that Sally, I understand how you must feel after looking after him all this time, walking and training him but the Jockey is a professional, he is trained to bring in the winners. You've done all you can for Charlie now sit back and let the jockey enjoy his race with him"

There was suddenly a bang as the starting gun went off and a great roar as the crowd of spectators rose all at once shouting for their respective horse to run, run, run.

The Colonel was almost beside himself jumping up and down shouting at Charlie to run faster. Charlie seemed to be in with a lot of horses about halfway round and didn't seem to be going as fast as he should. However, suddenly him and another horse came out of the crowd and raced towards the one that was in the lead. About three quarters of the way now and all three up in front were running as fast as they could, it looked as though they would all reach the finishing line together - then Champagne Charlie spurted forward - one length in front ot the others, goodness, two lengths in front now and he came into win three lengths in front.

The Colonel couldn't believe it, he sat down then he stood up, "did you see that my dear Bertha, he's won, he's won" he was so excited.

Sally and Christopher hugged each other, laughing out loud in their excitement.

Suddenly over the speakers came the announcement: - The winner of the third race was horse number three, Champagne Charlie.

Second - Little Runner - horse number seven.

Third - Fast Red - horse number four.

"Will the Owners and Trainer's come forward please?" Came the voice over the Loud Speaker.

"Go on darling" Mrs. Black gave the Colonel a gentle push, "take Sally, Christopher and I will wait here for you."

The jockey walked Champagne Charlie around the winning arena, the horse was snorting and sweating after his ordeal but he looked magnificent as he was walked around.

Charlie thought to himself, thank goodness I did it. Sally and Lady Jayne will so proud. Just then Sally came up and hugged him. Yes, she certainly was pleased, absolutely delighted. The crowd cheered as the Colonel was presented with a lovely Silver Cup that was to be his Trophy to keep.

Afterwards he proudly walked back and handed it without a word to Bertha, who was overwhelmed as she took it and sat down to brush away a tear.

* * *

The Race

14

Celebrations

Mr. and Mrs. Little watched the Colonel go back to his seat and followed him, pushing their way through the crowd. They had watched Champagne Charlie win with just as much excitement as the others.

Bertha and Rose put their arms around each other and hugged each other, laughing out loud at being so happy. Bertha showed Rose the beautiful silver trophy.

While this was happening Mr. Little was shaking the Colonel's hand till it nearly fell off, he was beaming all over his face and the Colonel was flushed red with pleasure.

Sally and Christopher were watching them all, both were grinning from ear to ear, they were so glad it worked out alright after all the trouble they had both caused.

Bertha suddenly invited them all back for a celebration cup of tea - "not on your life" burst out the Colonel - "it's Champagne or nothing!"

They all arrived back at the Black's place in their respective cars, then went outside onto the patio for the Celebration drink.

It was late afternoon now, still nice and warm, everyone was excited, talking about the three length's that Charlie had won by.

Bertha came out carrying a tray with the Champagne glasses on, plus a bottle the Colonel's best Champagne that he had been saving for such an occasion.

Colonel Black popped the cork and filled the glasses with the Bubbly, everyone helped themselves to a glass off of the tray.

"Here is a toast" beamed the Colonel, "to Champagne Charlie and his great win, may there be many more!"

"Here, here" they all chorused.

Then, Mr. and Mrs. Little looked at each other in a knowing way - "you tell them John" said Rose. "Tell us what?" asked Christopher.

"Well" said his Father slowly, "it's like this, it seems that Lady Jayne is going to be a Mother"

"A Mother" they all said together.

"That's right" went on Mr. Little. "Remember the Vet came today, well, that tummy trouble was what it turned out to be.

So, we shall have to give Lady Jayne special treatment, because this maybe the start of a new Super Breed"

"What do you mean by that John?" asked the Colonel.

"Well, looks like your Super Stallion who has just become a Winner is also going to become a Father later in the year"

"Can't be" said the Colonel going red.

"Certainly is" said his friend and neighbour.

Sally and Christopher couldn't believe their ears, "can we go and see her please?" asked Sally.

"Of course you can" said Mr. Little.

"Don't be long" the Colonel shouted, "Charlie will be back soon, you better break the news to him gently. Too much excitement in one day isn't good for him"

Sally hugged Lady Jayne and told her what a clever horse she was. However Lady Jayne didn't hear a word, she was off into one of her daydreams, dreaming of the new foal that the Vet had told her she was going to have in a few months time. She was wondering, would it be a Champagne colour like it's Father?

Lady Jayne had never been so happy, even the pain in her leg she hardly felt, now that she could dream of her new role of being a Mother. Yes, she was going to be a good Mother, she thought. So she couldn't wait to tell Charlie he was going to be a Father. But had to wait until she would be well enough to exercise with Christopher again when Sally would be exercising Champagne Charlie.

She daydreamed nearly every day of the moonlit night that they had galloped and galloped together, herself and Charlie. She knew now though, that dreams must stay dreams (like galloping to the end of the world).

She must live in the reality of today and be grateful for the love, food and good home that she is lucky enough to have.

Later that year -
Lady Jayne became the Proud Mother
of a beautiful Champagne coloured filly
which was named of all things - "Dark Tail"
you can probably guess why -
yes, she had a dark tail just like Lady Jayne - she was a real thoroughbred beauty.

THE WINNER
CHAMPAGNE CHARLIE

Champagne Charlie "Winner" after the race

THEY ARE A LOVELY FAMILY NOW

CHAMPAGNE CHARLIE

AND LADY JANE

WITH

DARK TAIL THEIR BEAUTIFUL FOAL.

www.ingramcontent.com/pod-product-compliance
Lightning Source LLC
Chambersburg PA
CBHW071843290426
44109CB00017B/1909